This book is dedicated to JoJo the Small Town Hound's people: Samantha, k, and Reilly, and to the wonderful citizens of the Town of Leesburg, especially the folks at Brick and Mortar Mercantile, Jock's Exxon, King Street Coffee, Coldwell Banker, and the Loudoun County Law Library who are very generous with their dog treats.

This is

JoJo

She's a friendly pup
with a unique hobby.

She loves exploring small towns, meeting their people, and learning their history.

She wrote this book to share one of her favorite places with you.

It was her idea, anyway.
Her humans typed it for her because, well,
keyboards are hard to use with paws.

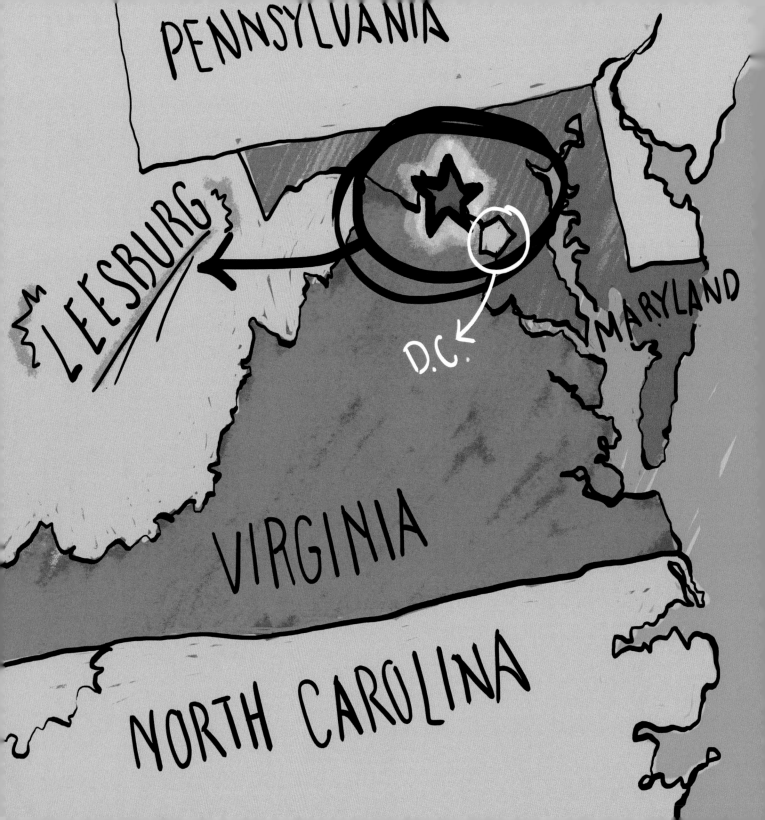

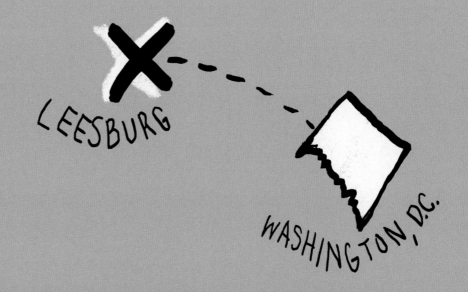

Leesburg, Virginia is in the northeastern part of the state, close to the Maryland and West Virginia borders, and 40 miles northwest of the Nation's Capital, Washington, D.C.

Leesburg is in Loudoun County, which has a courthouse with a great big lawn that's perfect for chasing squirrels!

JoJo wants everyone to know that the Law Library in the courthouse complex has dog treats available for all four-legged visitors.

The town was officially established by the
Assembly of Virginia in 1758.
That means there are more than 250 years of
different smells for good dogs to sniff
(that's nearly 2,000 dog years!)

It also means that the town has seen
a lot of American history.

Long ago, in the 1700's during the American Revolution, Loudoun County was home to the largest militia in Virginia, with over 1,700 residents taking up arms.

Later, after The War of 1812 began where the British invaded and threatened Washington, D.C.— The U.S. Constitution and The Declaration of Independence were hidden in Leesburg to keep them safe.

History doesn't tell us all the details, but JoJo's sources reported that very good doggos were in charge of guarding those important documents. Pretty cool, right?

JoJo was happy to learn those things about this town, but she really perked up when she found out about...

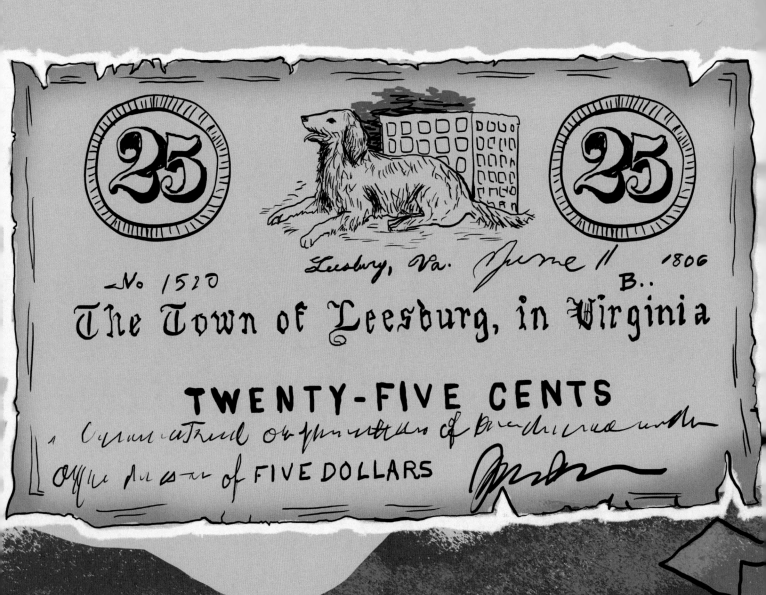

Because Leesburg is right on the border between the North and the South, the U.S. Civil War was a complicated time for this small town. Virginia was part of the Confederate States but like much of America the townspeople...

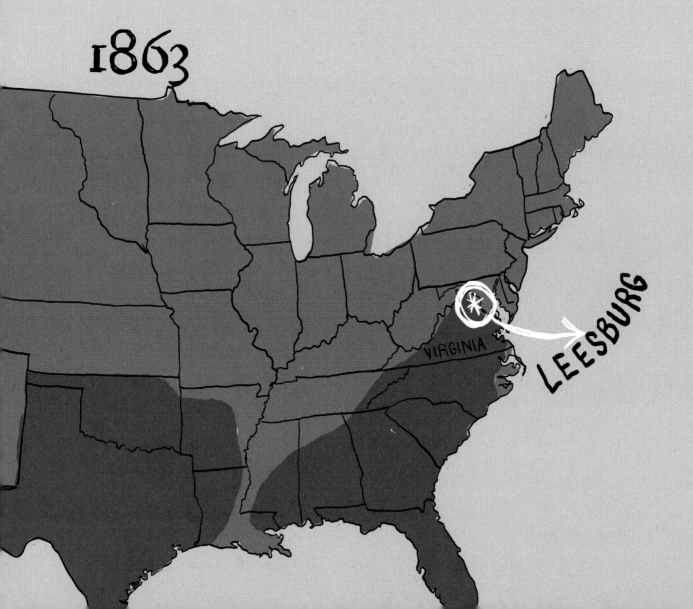

1863

VIRGINIA

LEESBURG

...were divided, with some serving in the Union Army and others in the Confederate Army.

Leesburg changed the kind of money used more than 150 times between 1861 and 1865 depending on who was in control of the town as the armies battled against each other.

This made it very confusing and difficult for townspeople to
know which kind of money to use.
So the town got creative and made up its own money.

A man named Martin Casey designed Leesburg's new currency. The town paid him $50 for his services, which would be worth $1,736 in today's dollars - that's a lot of pupper treats!

MARTIN CASEY

He must've really liked dogs, because the money he designed featured a large, shaggy, American Water Spaniel on each bill.

The townspeople loved the design, and named it Dog Money.

It may or may not be true that they howled like hounds when they exchanged money for goods and services, but JoJo thinks it happened that way.

Eventually, more than $93,000 worth of Dog Money was printed and distributed in Leesburg (awooooooo!).

If you ever make a trip to the town,
you can see actual Dog Money bills at the
Loudoun County Museum or the
Thomas Balch Library.

Both of those places are really close to Leesburg's historic downtown, where humans can shop, eat, get coffee, and visit art galleries and museums and pups can get lots of treats from friendly business owners.

And that's the story of the Curious Case of
Dog Money!

JoJo's pretty sure your hometown has some fun stories for her to discover - so keep the treats out and maybe she'll come for a visit!

If you'd like to learn more about the Town of Leesburg and its history, visit these websites (or better yet, visit the town itself so JoJo can give you big doggy kisses!):

https://ead.lib.virginia.edu/vivaxtf/view?docId=tbl/viletbl00069.xml

https://www.leesburgva.gov/departments/thomas-balch-library/research-reference-services/research-guides-book-indices/history-of-leesburg

https://historyimagined.wordpress.com/2018/03/09/leesburg-vas-dog-money

Made in the USA
Middletown, DE
16 April 2024

53088009R00020